THE NEST PRETTY LIFESTYLE GUIDE

MAKING SMALL CHOICES EVERY DAY THAT ADD UP TO A BEAUTIFUL LIFE!

HEIDI GAMMILL

Copyright © 2021 by Heidi Gammill

1st Edition

Copyright in Bradenton, Florida

All rights reserved.

No part of this book may be reproduced in any form or by any electronic or mechanical means, including information storage and retrieval systems, without written permission from the author, except for the use of brief quotations in a book review.

Paperback Print ISBN: 978-1-7369670-0-3

Hardcover Print: 978-1-7369670-3-4

E-book ISBN: 978-1-7369670-1-0

Illustrations by Susanna Booth

For permissions contact hello@heidigammill.com

CONTENTS

PART ONE
FOUNDATION

1. Nest Pretty — 3
2. Values — 7
3. Prioritizing — 11
4. Dreams — 15
5. Imaginations — 19
6. Elevating the Mundane to the Spectacular — 23
7. Positivity — 27
8. Simplicity — 31
9. Wellness — 35

PART TWO
GATEKEEPING

10. Your Home — 41
11. Your Emotions — 47
12. Your Mind and Spirit — 51

PART THREE
NESTING

13. Cleaning — 57
14. Organizing — 59
15. Systems — 61
16. Make it Pretty — 63
17. Share — 65
18. Nesting with Heart — 67
19. Nest Pretty is a Choice — 69

This book is dedicated to you, my dear friend!
And who you're aspiring to be! If you're anything like me, then you:

- Love the juxtaposition of proper vs. shocking
- Laugh a lot but mostly in your head
- Can't decide if you love technology or hate it
- Are organized but not a perfectionist
- Are working on being more polite and giving sincere compliments
- Love the sun
- Love to read . . . but rarely do
- Love to run . . . but rarely do
- Love to cook leisurely . . . but rarely do
- Love to smile at strangers
- Love to represent not just yourself but your God, your husband, your family, your truth
- Know perfection is not possible . . . right now
- Have learned the powerful truth: I am ENOUGH
- Don't dwell on yesterday
- Face the future with confidence and languish in the NOW
- Thrive on experiences not things and linger with the details
- Are positive and energetic
- Love to be with people who inspire you
- Love to teach

- Love to be alone
- Bookend your day with nostalgia: music and coffee, cocktail and music
- Recognize everything is value over price and time over money
- Recognize the power of choice and use it to your advantage
- Would rather shop where they ask your name and take the clothes from your arms than pile them into a cart and get frisked on the way into the dressing room
- Love to learn from everyone you meet
- Are overwhelmed, but you fake it until you make it
- Are open and closed, public and private
- Know you're powerful because you've done hard things
- Love to travel, and you love your own bed
- Love beautiful things

I see you!
XO

PART ONE
FOUNDATION

ONE

NEST PRETTY

Nest Pretty has been an inspiration for me, and I want it to be inspiring for you, too.

Nest Pretty v. The action of choosing to live your best life.

As I was contemplating a huge change in my life, I looked out of my window and saw a lovely sight—a nest. It was a beautifully crafted home for a family of sparrows.

Birds build nests not only to provide a landing spot for themselves, but also a place to raise and nurture a family. It's a place of beauty that's uniquely their own. No two nests are the same. It's fascinating to see the materials they use to make their homes, whether it be sticks, string, hair, straw, grass, or mud and the results are spectacular! Why am I telling you this?

I, too, have made it a practice to find things and use them to beautify my space and make my home a landing spot of fascination, details, and love. While I generally don't use sticks, string, hair, straw, grass, and mud, I'm not above using other people's "trash" to add a touch of entertainment and whimsy to my home.

I once found a painting in the garbage. It was a beautiful oil painting with a rich, heavy frame. Why was it in the trash? The canvas was torn in the center of the painting. To the former owners, it was ruined. To me, it was a flaw that didn't diminish the overall beauty of the piece. Rather, it reminded me of me. While my flaws may be glaring to others, I know I'm valuable, beautiful and loved.

So, what is Nest Pretty? It's a lifestyle. It's about valuing what you own . . . today. It's about valuing who you are . . . today. And it's about valuing who you want to be . . . today. Nest Pretty is **making small choices every day that add up to a beautiful life!**

What do I mean? It's about making decisions that bring you the most benefits and happiness. This does not mean you throw responsibility and obligations out the window. Instead, it's important to:

- Prioritize or do what's most important first, but then also remember to set time aside to do what you most enjoy.
- Keep your attitude positive and take pleasure in the simple things. Yet . . .
- Never settle for the mundane but do what you can to elevate every day to the spectacular!
- Become your life's editor-in-chief. If something's not working or serving a purpose, then get rid of it.

Nest Pretty is imagining a better use of your space, time, wardrobe, menu, chores, entertainment, and work.

Living the Nest Pretty Lifestyle is a choice!

It's choosing to:

- Design a life you love.

- Make life happen **for** you, instead of letting life happen **to** you.
- Control what you bring into your home — food, clothes, decor, cleaning supplies, and other household items — that ultimately either help or hinder your wellness journey.
- Educate yourself to do better and to be better.

Is it perfectionism? Never! It's a choice. You choose to live your best life ever and to enjoy every minute of it. Occasionally, I choose not to make my bed because I enjoy the feeling of freedom that it gives me more than I enjoy having a coiffed bed. Even though my bed is a wreck, it's *my choice* to leave it like that, so I'm still choosing to Nest Pretty.

It's a state of mind that helps you to live with a spirit of:

- Gratitude and appreciation
- Imagination and creativity
- Contentment and learning to work with what you have
- A desire to support your wellness, hormones and emotions so you can live your healthiest life

The beautiful thing about Nest Pretty is that every nest will be different and will reflect its own style, imagination, priorities, and values. No two nests will look the same. So, are you ready?

Let's break Nest Pretty down into three categories: 1) the decisions we make, 2) how our decisions affect our health and wellness, and 3) how our decisions affect our home and how we live.

Are you ready to begin **making small choices every day that add up to a beautiful life?** Then let's do this! And let's make your life Nest Pretty!

TWO

VALUES

What are your values? Values are important and lasting beliefs or ideals, the standards or principles by which we live.

Establishing your values is the first step to all other decisions because they have a major influence on our behavior and attitude. They serve as a guide in all situations and should be non-negotiable.

Do you lack values, wish you had more, or don't like the ones you have? Then, start exploring what's most important to you. Is it your spirituality, your family, your friends? Since values are the very foundation of our lives, this is a good time to review your values, standards, and priorities as you prepare to Nest Pretty.

Being clear on the principles you live by will help you to decide where to start. Choose ONE to work on and weave it into your nest. I'll give you an example:

One of my values is taking care of my health. It's an essential aspect of my quality of life. I do my best to control what I put in and on my body. Because I value myself, I know that when I'm healthy, I can do anything! I feel invincible, and I'm able to move, sleep, and be very productive. So, taking care of my health is a non-negotiable, and every choice I make should support this standard in my life.

What about you? Do you value your health? What choices have you made to support that decision?

This is just one example of value in my life. Taking care of my health allows me to live the best life possible. Unfortunately, when it comes to life there's not much we can control, but we do have choices. The choices we make, will affect our health for better or worse, based on how we decide to care for ourselves.

Healthy habits start with good choices. What can you choose to do every day to show that you value your health? Consider three small choices you can make that can have a big impact on your health:

1. Drink lots of water
2. Get 6-8 hours of sleep
3. Exercise

Are these no-brainers or a HUGE lifestyle change? If one or more of these choices seem impossible to achieve, start smaller. Whether our health will thrive, or dive comes down to the small choices we make, every day so build up to the larger goal by starting with more manageable ones.

For example, if drinking eight 8-ounce glasses of water is a challenge, then start with four glasses. Or you can grab a 32-ounce bottle and decide you will drink it before you get home from work. Start small and work your way up.

Is getting enough sleep difficult? Set an alarm to remind you when you need to start winding down. Program your TV to go off at a certain time. If exercising is not your thing, just take 10 minutes, in the morning, at lunch, or as soon as you get home from work to walk around your neighborhood or office. Go to the mall, park or the beach and walk around there. Start small and make it enjoyable. Make it something you look forward to doing, or you won't do it at all.

There are literally a thousand other things that you can do to improve your health. However, thousands of choices generally result in overwhelm; it can lead to decision fatigue and could eventually cause you to give up. If you find three new habits overwhelming, then just choose one thing to do and work up from there. Everyone can handle choosing ONE thing to improve their life.

Once you've mastered those three things and they become habits, make three more small choices that will help you work towards your goal or choose another of your core values to work on.

VALUE SCALE—

What's most important to you? Do you know how to assess your values?

If they teach this in school, then I missed it! A few years ago, my husband and I were faced with a sudden change in circumstances, and we knew we'd have to move out of state. We wanted to make a good decision and love where we were going to live because, as you well know, moving is no joke!

So, we made a list of the top five places we'd like to settle. Some places we put down because of family and friends. Others were based purely on weather and my quick search of which states have the lowest percentage of overcast days — something I value in order to maintain my quality of life.

Below each choice, we made a list of pros and cons. It was overwhelming! We had a list but still hadn't made a decision until my 15-year-old nephew Connor looked at our list and said, "This means nothing unless you put values next to your pros and cons."

That led us to take a second look at our list and assign values to each item, hence the value scale. Next to each pro, we rated how important it was to us on a scale of 1-10. We did the same with the cons. Before we knew it, our choices were narrowed down to two places that tied on the value scale, and it was just a matter of how courageous we were to make our decision.

Based on how our values were prioritized, we made our choice, and we didn't look back. We're both so happy that we knew what was most important to us when it came time to decide which direction our life was going to take.

Now, it's your turn. What do you value? Step one is to make your list of values (you should have more than one). On a scale of 1-10, where do your values sit? Step two is to prioritize your values. How do you know which ones should be your priority?

NEST PRETTY EXERCISE:

Pick a value that's most important to you, get creative, imagine a plan and choose three things you can do today to make it happen. GO!

Grab your Nest Pretty Resource here:

THREE

PRIORITIZING

Our whole life is all about priorities. When you get out of bed, what do you do first? Do you brush your teeth, take a shower, or start the coffee? All of those habits are necessary, but the one you do first is your priority.

Nest Pretty focuses on making small choices every day that help to create a beautiful life for you and your family. Attaining our dreams and goals are a very big part of having a happy and fulfilling life. While part of this means we get to do what we want, there will always be needs and obligations that can't be ignored.

Successfully juggling these two things — our wants and our obligations — requires us to figure out what our priorities are and to give them the proper attention. Our goals and values can be hard to attain or maintain, when we have too much clutter in our life.

How do you know if it's time to declutter and reprioritize? Ask yourself: Am I super busy, always on-the-go, always doing but not accomplishing much? Do I have big goals that I want to reach but don't know where to begin?

Prioritizing can be summed up this way: **Do what's**

most important first, and then you can do what you most enjoy.

So, let's begin by prioritizing our values. In the previous chapter, we talked about assigning a meaning to our values. Let's start with the value that had the highest number of points and call that your first priority.

What's your ultimate goal to attain or maintain that value? Think about it. What does your big picture look like? What's your endgame? It's true, when we look at the big picture, it can be overwhelming. But like a work of art, the finished product is usually accomplished one brushstroke at a time.

It helps to know what your goal is in order to begin prioritizing the baby steps you will need to take to get there.

Find a quiet place in your home, somewhere you will not be interrupted. If you regularly take time for yourself, you may only have to sit quietly for a few minutes before the ideas start flowing. I'm not going to lie—we are all more overstimulated in this smartphone and tablet age than we realize, including me. So, the first time you do this, it'll take time and undistracted stillness (without an electronic device) to get clarity.

So, find your spot, grab a comfy chair and a journal so that you're able to think about and answer the following questions:

- What value is most important to you? (faith, family, finances, physical or mental health for example) Is it obvious to you what your number one priority is?
- What is your goal for that value?
- Are you actively working towards attaining your goal?
- What's working and what's not working?
- What could you be doing with your time and resources to better work at attaining that goal?

- What steps do you need to take to make that happen?

These questions aren't always easy to answer. That's why you need time and uninterrupted quiet. Once you're able to really focus, it's time to put your pen to paper. Write it all down. Honestly answering the questions above will help you to start hammering out the details as to how you can get to your ultimate goal. Meditating on how your goal will help you to enjoy your life may also give you the impetus to follow through.

Are there any baby steps along the way that you can put on autopilot? In the same way that brushing your teeth, taking a shower, and starting the coffee every morning happens without thinking about them, you may have some things on your list that you can do every day that are no-brainers.

Or perhaps there are things that will need to be done daily or frequently. Can you put them on your schedule as non-negotiables, so you never have to think twice? Doing so will free up mental and emotional energy to put towards your obligations *and* what you enjoy doing while still actively pursuing your goals.

If you are still having difficulty clearly defining your priorities and goals, take a few moments, every day, in your quiet place journaling and asking yourself questions until you can narrow it down.

Just remember, Nest Pretty is about making small choices, so there's no need to get overwhelmed! You're the designer of your life. Only you know your goals. Only you are the dreamer of your dreams. And Nest Pretty is the way your dreams become reality.

. . .

NEST PRETTY EXERCISE: Choose ONE priority or goal. Pick one thing you can do today and choose to make it happen. GO!

FOUR

DREAMS

Have you stopped dreaming? I'm not talking about what your subconscious does when you're asleep. I'm talking about the dreams you had when you were a child. The dreams you had about what you would do or what you would be if you had a choice. Was it in high school? College? When you started a family?

I recently listened to a millennial talk about her work and how much she loved it.

She said she was "living the dream." Her advice to others was to do something they "love to do" too.

Our parents' generation did what that they HAD to do. Their jobs were generally mundane, obligatory, and almost always a challenge to be endured. It can be difficult to break that mold especially once we have a family of our own. Life is filled with obligations and we often feel stuck, not able to make the choices we want.

That's why living a Nest Pretty Lifestyle is so important — because we all have a choice. We make choices every day. Those choices can either improve our life and make it beautiful, or they can make it a challenge to be endured. So, my question for you is this: do you still allow yourself to dream of the possibilities — to dream of doing what you want to do, instead of always doing what you have to do?

Better yet, when was the last time you allowed yourself to voice a dream. To decide, 'I LOVE THIS'? It's hard to believe that what used to be a normal pastime when we were children now requires scheduling, self-control, and more than that, **courage**. It requires courage to say. "I LOVE THIS," or "I prefer that" or "this is my favorite, and I want more of it in my life." It takes courage to be different and not to settle for what everyone else is doing or what everyone else tells us we should like.

When we were young and someone asked us what we wanted to be when we grew up, we had no problem telling them what we dreamed of becoming. We were proud of our dreams. Perhaps you were like my husband, who confidently and unapologetically declared, "I want to be a hooker man!" His parents' relief didn't come until hours later when they were driving through town and their son pointed to a tow truck and cried out "Hooker Man!" Phew!

Regardless of our choices when we were younger, we didn't rationalize, reason, explain, or make excuses. We just said it. Whether or not it was practical didn't matter! We weren't afraid of what others would think. It was what we wanted to be, OUR dream, and no one was going to take that away from us.

If someone asked our favorite color, animal, type of music, or sports, we didn't overanalyze our answer, we didn't fear judgment. We just told people what our favorite was. After all, there was no right or wrong answer to those questions. They were a matter of choice.

Now that we're adults, it's still a matter of choice and preference. Why do we care more now about what people think than we did then? We should still allow ourselves to dream, to have favorites, to be what we want to be. We should have the courage to tell others. Why? When giving voice to our dreams,

THE NEST PRETTY LIFESTYLE GUIDE

it encourages us and gives us the impetus to work toward them. It makes us accountable when we share our dreams with others. We will not be allowed to forget them or sweep them under the carpet because others know and will remind us. These dreams will be with us until we make them come true.

As you lay your foundation for a Nest Pretty Lifestyle, I encourage you to channel your bold and unapologetic six-year-old and proclaim your dreams!

NEST PRETTY EXERCISE:

Write it down, put your dreams on paper, the more details the better. This helps you to commit, but it's super powerful when you go back and see that they all came true.

And then, I double dog dare you to say them out loud! Pick a trusted friend to confide your dreams in.

FIVE

IMAGINATIONS

Peace and quiet are illusive necessities for those who want their imaginations to thrive. Nowadays, we're so overly stimulated that we feel like we don't have time or the ability to just stop and think. But I've found that it's in those fleeting moments of deafening quiet and peaceful stillness, that my mind finds its greatest inspiration.

I used to go home every day during my lunch hour. As I waited for my food to warm in the oven, I would sit in my space and just look around. No music playing, no TV on, no iPad or iPhone in my hand. I would just sit in the quiet, observe, and enjoy my surroundings. It was then that I could truly appreciate what I loved, what was working, or what I needed to get rid of.

Sometimes, my deliberate contemplation would cause me to get up and rearrange a bookshelf, picture frames, or even my furniture. But more often, it was in the silence that I would be rewarded with some of my most fantastical inspirations.

One gorgeous, warm summer day, as I was sitting and musing in the noiseless calm, I imagined how much I would love to have a balcony. How wonderful it would be to enjoy the beauty of the outdoors right outside of our apartment! At the time, we were living in a 450 square foot, 1 bedroom, 1 bath apartment, so at first, it didn't seem possible. But that's when I was hit with a vision!

> **"Imagination is everything. It is the preview of life's coming attractions."**
> — **Albert Einstein**

There was an area in my building where people would drop off unwanted clothes or furniture. In that moment, as I was imagining my balcony, I remembered seeing two smallish dining room chairs there. I left my food in the oven and ran to see if they were still there. They were! I brought them back and began to set up my "balcony."

I decided the bedroom was the perfect spot. So, I set the two chairs on the side of our bed by our window that overlooked the busy, sunny, fabulous walkway lined with ever-changing maple trees. I opened the window and screen. Voila! A balcony! There was just enough space for Judah and I to sit with our favorite beverage. I could stretch my legs out and prop my feet up on the windowsill. At certain times of the day, my skin could be warmed by the sun. How fab!

We loved enjoying our first cup of espresso in the morning or a martini at sunset there. I also loved the whimsy of inviting my family or friends to join me for a glass of wine on my "balcony" and then having them assist me in heckling the passers-by (that we knew and loved) as they walked past. Hours of entertainment for the price of my imagination!

There was another time, right after Judah had been declared gluten free by his doctor, that I decided I needed a pantry. The thought of figuring out how to feed him with a plethora of new and exotic flours and alternatives, frankly, rocked my world. I knew it was going to lead to more staples in the cupboards, and I didn't have the space for that.

So, one day, during a quiet moment of musing, I dreamed

of a pantry. I grabbed a pen and paper and drew it out. I included in the drawing a special place for all of the small appliances that were about to earn their place in my kitchen. The shelves for new exotic flours I was going to buy and other healthy options that would be a must.

I labored over the drawings for my entire lunch hour . . . with a ruler. My dream was precise. Once I was done dreaming, imagining, and drawing, I showed Judah. I told him that this was our new dream pantry. He didn't seem as excited as I was, but that didn't matter.

The crazy thing was, shortly after imagining and drawing what I wanted, I saw IT! Well, actually, I walked right by it. "IT" was a hideous armoire in the ugliest color possible. I had a "cartoon moment" where I did a rubber-necking double-take and realized my dream pantry was right in front of me! All it needed was a coat of paint, some molding, and lights installed inside. It was perfect. And all it took was a moment of deafening quiet, peaceful stillness, and a little imagination.

NEST PRETTY EXERCISE:

Find a quiet space. Set a timer. Turn off or put away all electronic devices. Sit quietly with a pen and paper. Observe and imagine the possibilities.

SIX

ELEVATING THE MUNDANE TO THE SPECTACULAR

We were invited to an open mic event. Anyone who wanted to participate could come up to the stage to read a poem, sing a song, or play an instrument. My sister and her family happened to be visiting at the time, and I mentioned that if they wanted to participate, they could. My five-year-old niece, Jana, decided she wanted to do something. After looking all over our apartment, she found Judah's old recorder from grade school and set to learning it.

An hour later, to our surprise, she walked right up to the master of ceremonies and declared that she wanted to go first! When she was asked the name of her piece, she announced "Jana's Flute Spectacular!" Her confidence amazed me, and I realized that this was such a great lesson. In life, we can be bystanders or participants. Which one was I? Which one are you?

Why do I bring this up? Because our lives are filled with mundane activities, many of which we do daily: cook, eat, exercise, work, clean the house, sleep, etc. Sometimes, they become so routine that we don't even realize just how bored we really are. How can you turn a mundane, routine activity into something spectacular?

Let's take just one daily task that could easily be described as dull and see what we can do to elevate it into something exciting.

Breakfast — this has often been described as the most important meal of the day. Why? Because our body has been working off the energy stores that our last meal gave us, the previous night. What we eat and how we eat as we break our fast can set the tone for our entire day.

Do you sit down to eat, or do you rush through it? Do you eat on the go? Is what you eat healthy, or is it fast food? Do you eat carbs along with your venti caramel latte? Is it only a smoothie? Has breakfast become so routine that you don't even care what you put in your mouth as long as it doesn't impact the last few moments you spend hugging your pillow?

To turn something mundane into a spectacular event requires planning, thought, and time. Not a lot, just a little, but it's totally worth it. Here are just a few suggestions:

1. Eat only what you love. Plan a capsule menu of your favorite foods that will help motivate you to get out of bed.
2. Serve it on your fine china, if you have some. Most people don't have fine china like our mothers used to. However, if you do have it, why not use it? Otherwise, it will just sit there collecting dust and no one else will use it either. I understand if you don't want to break your good china. You most likely won't. If you do, it's no biggie and you may be able to find a replacement! Your life, your joy, and your health matter, more than things!
3. Make it fancy. Fold your napkins instead of just putting them on the table. Put thought and care into the presentation. It's a small detail, but details

are so important and make life worth savoring. Oh, and by the way, you're worth it!
4. Show up. Get out of bed 15 minutes earlier and enjoy breakfast with your family. Make it a tradition, a ritual, a slow and steady way to greet your day, your family, and your nutrition.

Making any one of those small choices could help you turn a mundane, boring breakfast into something meaningful and spectacular. Living your life beautifully — even in the small details — is just one way you can elevate the ordinary into the extraordinary.

> *"Attention to detail is not about perfection. It's about excellence, about constant improvement." — Chris Denny*

Let's not stop there. The list I had at the beginning of this chapter — cook, eat, exercise, work, clean the house, sleep — I'll give you one thing in each activity you can do today that can turn this routine into something you WANT to do.

- Cook — Prepare a capsule menu of all of your favorite dishes, ones you love to eat and prepare. GO!
- Eat — Plate everything up gourmet style before it hits the table. It's all about presentation. GO!
- Sleep — Get the spa music and diffuser going an hour before bed, heavy on the lavender essential oil. GO!
- Exercise — Blast that song that motivates you to

push through those push-ups or squats. Then do five more. GO!
- Work — Set a goal for yourself, one that's reachable, but one that excites you. GO!
- Clean the house — Get your favorite playlist going and set out a reward for yourself that you can have when you're done — a glass of champagne, a piece of decadent chocolate, or set aside time for a bubble bath. GO!

One thing, one little tweak, may be all that's needed to turn the mundane into the spectacular and that boring breakfast into something memorable. Now, it's your turn. Your **Nest Pretty Challenge** is to find one thing in your life, your home, your routine and do one thing to elevate it from mundane into spectacular.

Remember my niece, Jana, and her spontaneous "flute spectacular." Seize the moment and make a change! Turn the mundane into the spectacular.

In life, we can be bystanders or participants. Which one are you?

SEVEN

POSITIVITY

How we think makes us who we are. Negative thinking attracts negative energy; positive thinking attracts positive energy. We create our thoughts that become our reality. If we go into a situation with a negative thought process, then we are almost sure to have a negative outcome.

Negativity is contagious, but so is positivity. Both spread quickly and easily. Negativity damages those who subscribe to it. Positivity encourages, uplifts, and it's healing to the soul. It's a constant struggle to stay positive, but it's possible. That's why it's one of the cornerstones of a Nest Pretty Lifestyle. Positivity, like negativity, is a choice; it begins with a thought.

For example: "My home is beautiful." Think it — believe it — and it will be so. Why? Because if you think your home is beautiful, you'll take pride in your home. You'll keep it clean, organized, and well-appointed. It will be beautiful.

Or perhaps it's more personal, like "I'm having a bad hair day." Think it — believe it — and it will be so. Why? Because no matter what you try, your hair will never live up to your expectations. And every time you pass a mirror, that's going to be all you see. You'll have bad hair.

Negative thoughts are easy to come by; all we have to do is

turn on the news. But positive thoughts are worth fighting for because they make the world a better place to live and add to our inner joy. It's that simple. How do you feel when someone takes the time to smile at you, compliment you, tell you they're happy you're here? Try it! The next time you go to the store, bank, or a restaurant, give the person serving you a kind smile, a genuine compliment, or a sincere 'thank you.' Nine times out of 10, that person will not be able to hold themselves back from smiling in return.

Only you can choose how you're going to think or how you'll react to what life throws at you. So how can you make positive thinking your default choice every day?

First, choose to focus your mind on something inspiring, motivating, encouraging, and uplifting every day. Begin and end your day with asking yourself the following:

- What's going right today?
- What's making me happy?
- What am I grateful for?
- What am I thankful for?

Remember, negativity and guilt may motivate for a moment, but positivity, encouragement, and love will motivate for a lifetime.

Second, choose to slow down. Our lives are so hectic, we may not have time to think about what positive things are happening in our lives. Sometimes, we need to slow down in order to move forward. Slowing down is a choice that can lead to greater appreciation for life and a greater level of happiness.

Third, choose to stop worrying and start living "in the moment." This allows us to escape from adversity and undue anxiety, while conserving our inner energy. Living in the moment doesn't mean we don't care about the future. It means that when we make a choice to do something, we're able to focus solely on doing it, rather than letting our mind wander into the future (or the past).

Fourth, choose to practice gratitude. This is the key to positive thinking because it forces you to focus on the good things happening in your life. A good way to get into this practice is by writing down 3-5 things every day in a gratitude journal. Writing these things down is an exercise that trains your brain to look for positive things, even if they're small, to take the focus off of what may not be the best of situations.

And finally, choose to practice cleanliness. When what we have around us is kept neat and clean, it affects our mood and our stress levels and that of our family in positive ways. Instead of apologizing to your company, family, or even to yourself about a room, a table, or a corner, choose to move forward and fix it, clean it, or organize it. Stop apologizing and act. Our home is our refuge, so make it a haven of positivity!

I'll admit, it can be really difficult to stay positive in the face of adversity and failure. However, when you choose to be positive, it can enable you to develop a mental attitude that will allow you to adapt more easily even when enduring unexpected and unwanted changes in your life. After all, success and happiness do not come from always avoiding or escaping the challenges that find you. Instead, developing positive personality traits and a positive attitude will help you to cope with and overcome the harsh realities of life.

Here are a couple of personal challenges if you find your brain has a 7-lane highway of negativity:

1. Choose to be your own cheerleader. Positive and optimistic people have learned to cheer themselves on even when everyone else is booing.
2. Choose to see the good in others. Sincerely commend and compliment them.

It's going to feel amazing. I promise. I'm not telling you to be an annoying Pollyanna who sees the world through rose-colored glasses. No, be real and be positive.

Be Real Positive.

NEST PRETTY EXERCISE:

Cleaning and organizing your home can help you and your family be more positive about the space in which you live. So, try this — choose to throw just one thing away:

- Junk mail
- Old tennis shoes that you haven't worn in a year
- All of those Amazon boxes

How did that feel? Good? Great? That feeling is so easy to duplicate, and it actually may become addicting to throw something else away, remove items that don't belong, wipe the dust, vacuum the floor, and reimagine your space.

Don't do all of these things at once. Choose one thing and do it. The next day, do another thing. Reward yourself for the positive action you're taking and the positivity that you're adding to the space. Open the blinds and let the sun in and fill your home with feel-good botanicals!

EIGHT

SIMPLICITY

"Simplicity boils down to two steps: Identify the essential. Eliminate the rest."
— **Leo Babauta**

The words in the quote above are at the very heart of living a Nest Pretty Lifestyle. Nest Pretty is about simplifying and editing — your home, your closet, your systems, your life. If something is not working for you or is complicating your life, then get rid of it! If you're not able to get rid of it, then can you imagine how to improve whatever it is that's impeding your ability to streamline your world?

Simplicity is the opposite of complicated. Sound oversimplified? Let's think about it:

- If your decor is simple, it's easier to clean your home.
- If your wardrobe is simple, it's easier to get dressed in the morning.

- If you simplify your menu, the question, 'what's for dinner?' becomes non-existent.
- If you simplify your laundry routine, you can get it done every week without excuses.

There are so many things we do daily and weekly that you can simplify to make your life easier and live the life you want to live. For example, think about how you could simplify your bills, bookkeeping, plants, pet care, cars, routines.

The more we simplify our lives, the more we can focus on who and what we value the most — our mates, our kids, or our friends.

> ***"Life is really simple,***
> ***But we insist on complicating it."***
> ***— Confucius***

If your life is super complicated and leaves you overwhelmed, stressed, and feeling like you're spinning out of control. The best decision you can make is to simplify. Look hard at what's going on in your life? What's making it complicated? What's stressing you out? What do you have to keep? What can you eliminate?

Remember, it took time to complicate matters, so it'll take time to simplify. Simplifying won't happen overnight.

You may need to map it out, plan it out, create a list or two or three. Journal to figure out who you are and what you want out of a more simplified life. Start by identifying the complicated, so that you know exactly what you need to eliminate.

- Make a list of action steps needed to get there.
- Choose one thing to do at a time.
- If you try to juggle multiple goals, you could end up paralyzed and never accomplish anything.

- Pick one thing on your list. Do it. Then, move onto the next.

***"The plans of the diligent surely lead to success,
But all who are hasty surely head for poverty."
— Proverbs 21:5***

Edit, edit, edit.

Doing one thing at a time may seem like the slow way to go, but you'll be surprised at how quickly your focus will take you through your list of to-dos.

I was once asked if constantly editing my life was exhausting. My answer was and still is 'no.' I love to re-evaluate my life and refine my home, my closet, my schedule, and my systems. Finding something that doesn't work for me and either fixing it or getting rid of it isn't exhausting — it's energizing! Why? Because it's empowering! I'm in control of my life; my life isn't controlling me. You can do the same by editing what doesn't work for you.

Let's say you bought a pair of shoes. They're so adorable, the perfect little "Barbie" shoe, strappy with high heels. But the first time you put them on, they are super uncomfortable. You keep them, thinking that they'll stretch out, but the second and third time you wear them your feet, legs, knees and back ache terribly. How long would it be before you figured out the shoes were a problem? Would it even take you until the third time?

Once you realize it's the cutie-patootie shoes that are causing you pain, then it's a matter of valuing yourself, your health, and your well-being over whatever emotional pull these cute shoes have on your heart and getting rid of them.

That's an easy one. However, not all of our issues or problems are so obvious. Identifying the culprit may take time and may only be found after a process of elimination.

This is what I know to be true: When you can identify the

problem, it becomes easier to see the solution. Brainstorm with the family to get ideas if they don't come easy for you. Then use your imagination, keep your eyes open, and wait. You may get a fantastic idea when you least expect it, which is so much fun and very Nest Pretty!

"Have nothing in your house that you do not know to be useful or believe to be beautiful."
— ***William Morris***

NEST PRETTY EXERCISE:
 Curl up in your usual comfy chair with your favorite beverage. Use your imagination to visualize what it would look and feel like to simplify. Write your ideas down. Choose one thing to do today.

As you continue to put this into action, be prepared to put in consistent effort. It takes time, and it takes work. And remember, never be too proud to ask for help.

NINE

WELLNESS

Our health and wellness are things we take for granted until they're gone. The climb back can be arduous, expensive, exhausting, and discouraging. It's best not to lose your health in the first place.

I lost my wellness in 2006 and was diagnosed with an autoimmune disease.

Immune system disorders cause either abnormally low activity or over activity of the immune system. In cases of immune system overactivity, the body attacks and damages its own tissues. These are called autoimmune diseases.

Immune deficiency diseases lower the body's ability to fight invaders, causing vulnerability to infections. In cases like mine, in response to an unknown trigger, the immune system may begin producing antibodies that, instead of fighting infections, attack the body's own tissues.

With that diagnosis, my life changed forever. In retrospect, I wish it would've happened sooner. Why? Because so much wisdom, self-awareness, and empathy came from my experience. I learned so much about my body, but the part that's stayed with me, and I'm reminded of daily, is that our choices and actions have consequences. These can affect our life for the positive or the negative.

What we bring into our home, put into our mouths, and use on our bodies has a cost.

I was shocked when I learned that the average American woman uses hundreds of chemicals on her skin per day! At that time, I was one of those women!

I'd never thought about it nor considered the harmful effects. I assumed that if it was on the store shelves, it wouldn't harm me — it was safe, it was approved.

Constant exposure to harmful toxins can have a cumulative effect on the body. It may get to the point where your body proclaims, "enough is enough!" Like mine did.

As I did more and more research on my condition, I realized that as the gatekeeper of my household, I'm responsible for the decisions that could benefit or harm my family.

Frankly, I was overwhelmed. I had to make drastic changes and fast — from my diet to my lifestyle.

I was drowning in a sea of desperation, but even then, I was keenly aware of this one irrefutable truth: I can only control ME. My choices, my actions, my reactions. And so, I set to determining what was within my control in order to benefit and support my body while it healed.

My list included practical steps, activities, attitudes, habits, and restrictions. I gave myself the permission to endure with grace and dignity. With my hubby's help, we implemented several strategies:

- Eliminating all nonessentials that resulted in stress
- Requesting help when needed
- Controlling the controllable
- Sleeping more (including a tuck-in)

Even just having the word "restriction" in my vocabulary was liberating. 'No' became my favorite, most powerful word.

If you've never gone on a "no diet," you should. I highly recommend it! It's SO freeing!

Then, I focused on losing the chemicals in my life. This didn't happen overnight. It was a process of trial and error. I tried a lot of DIYs and made some expensive mistakes. I was willing to spend the money but finding products or self-care routines that I loved took a lot of time and research.

I finally found a company that worked for me and made my chemical-free life easier to manage. They literally took the guesswork out of the last pieces to my chemical-free puzzle of natural products that I loved. Yes, with this decision, there was a cost. For me, it was a decision well-made and money well-spent.

Why am I telling you this? Because every decision you make has a cause and effect — your actions have consequences. If your choices are adversely affecting your wellness, what will you do to change that? What are you willing to give up to improve your health and wellness? That decision will have a cost and a direct impact on your Nest Pretty Lifestyle.

NEST PRETTY EXERCISE:

Switch and ditch. Switch out one chemical-laden product (make-up, household cleaner, your favorite room deodorizer) for something natural and chemical-free.

PART TWO
GATEKEEPING

TEN

YOUR HOME

A gatekeeper is someone who controls access to someone or something. They decide who is let in and who stays outside the gate. Back in the day, this was a position of trust and came with heavy accountability. The lives of all those behind the gate depended on the gatekeeper to keep them safe from enemy combatants. If a gatekeeper was found asleep on the job, they were stripped, beaten, and paraded around in front of all the people. It was a humiliating example and reminder that this responsibility was not to be taken lightly.

Nowadays, the term "gatekeeper" is used metaphorically to describe someone standing by a "point of entry," guarding against anything unwanted coming through. The term applies to those in business, the music industry, social media, etc. But it can also apply to those who decide on the foods and goods that come into a home.

Being the gatekeeper for a family is also a huge responsibility. I am the gatekeeper for my family; you are the gatekeeper for yours. The health and security of our family depend on us. We decide what our family watches on TV, what clothing they wear, and the food they eat. We also decide which soap, shampoo and household cleaners we use.

That means that we are culpable for the toxins and chemicals we choose to bring in and daily expose our family to. The entertainment our family consumes is with our permission. It also means that the bag of sour cream and onion potato chips in your pantry didn't magically show up last week. And the freezer didn't beam that container of Ben & Jerry's Cherry Garcia directly from the grocery store. No one believes that these items were crouching in a dark corner of the grocery cart and leapt into your trunk. They didn't scale the walls of the house in the middle of the night. No Ms. Gatekeeper — you unlocked the gate, threw the doors wide open, and let them set up camp!

So, ask yourself: What am I allowing inside my gate? What am I allowing my family to feed on mentally, physically, emotionally? Is it what's best for them or just the most convenient for me? What are the long-term effects of the choices I'm making on their behalf? Are my decisions promoting the health and happiness of my family?

No one can do this job perfectly, so please don't try. Nest Pretty is about making *choices*. Good choices that add up to a beautiful life. So, let's talk about just a few choices you can make that will help you to be a better gatekeeper for your family.

Plan Ahead. *Ohhhh man! But planning takes time!* Yes, I know. Stop your whining. The amount of time it takes you to whine and complain about how much time something is going to take is enough time to actually plan something on your list.

Don't believe me? Let's try it. Get out your stopwatch and whine after me: *"Oooooh man! But planning takes time I don't have!"* Did you time it? Great! Now, say this next sentence out loud and time it: *"Let's watch a documentary on Netflix tonight."* Hmm, I don't know what your stopwatch said, but mine told me that it took twice as much time to whine about planning as it was to actually plan wholesome entertainment for the family.

Granted, that was an easy one. Let's choose something

more challenging: Planning a menu. Now, this definitely takes time, especially if you also do what I do and plan out your grocery list at the same time. But what's the alternative? Do you have time to wait for meat to defrost? Do you have time to make last minute trips to the grocery store? How many times have you rushed home to frantically make dinner only to find out that you don't have all the ingredients? All that time you didn't have to "plan" you are now wasting either at the store (delaying dinner), changing the meal (delaying dinner), or ordering in (delaying dinner).

Let's face it, we're all so busy that by the time you get home, your family is already hungry. Any time that's wasted makes it more and more unlikely that you'll be able to keep them away from that bag of sour cream & onion potato chips. By the time dinner is made or the pizza guy gets there, their tummies are full of monounsaturated and trans fats. So, the salad you (might) make will have minimal impact on their health.

The moral of the story — plan ahead. The hour it will take you every week to plan a menu and make your grocery list will save you HOURS of worry, extra and unnecessary trips to the store, desperate calls to the pizza guy, and missed opportunities to follow through on your decision to be a better gatekeeper.

Do Your Research. This goes for everything — food, entertainment, social media, household cleaners, etc. Everything that is allowed to come into your home should be thoroughly vetted and examined. READ THE LABELS. If a show is rated TV-14, why? If a bottle is labeled "natural," is it? If our food says it's "organic" or "grass fed," what does that really mean?

You have to ask yourself these questions and look for the answers. People will tell you what they think you want to hear. That's because they're running a business and are concerned about their bottom line. You're the gatekeeper for your home.

You're concerned about the safety, health, and welfare of your family. That is YOUR bottom line. You have to prove to yourself the reasons why you think a product has earned an important place next to the ones you love the most. You can't put that responsibility on anyone else.

Decide once and follow through. Decision fatigue is real. It occurs when people feel exhausted from making too many choices or, if I may be so bold, when we make the *same decision* again and again and again. Avoid this by deciding once and following through.

Once you decide to plan your menu in advance, don't let anything distract you or take away that hour. Once you decide to eat healthy, don't bring Ben and Jerry into the house when you know that in a moment of desperation or depression, you'll immediately seek solace in their sweet company. Once you decide that a TV show or movie is inappropriate for the kids, don't let them watch it anyway because little Johnny's parents let him watch it. Once you decide that a chemical is doing your family more harm than good, don't buy another bottle just because it's on sale. Once you decide that the kids have to show you their social media accounts or turn their phones in before they go to bed, don't let them wear you down with their insistence on privacy.

Gatekeepers in ancient times were warriors, the first line of defense for a city. It was a position of trust and responsibility. Decide once and don't think about it again. Just follow through. Life is too short to spend it vacillating as to what you should or should not do. Plan ahead, do your research, decide once. Keep your family safe, secure, and healthy.

Nest Pretty Challenge: Make a menu for the week with an accompanying grocery list. Post it in a place for the family to see.

Consider what you've allowed into your home this week and if it's serving you and making you stronger.

1. Food & drink
2. Supplements
3. Body care products

What you use to:

- Clean your teeth and hair
- Enhance your beauty
- Protect your skin from the sun and insects
- Clean your clothes and house
- Make your house smell amazing

Because I care about the health of my family, I made a choice that has upped my confidence in knowing that what we're using as a family is benefitting us and giving our bodies the tools we need to thrive, not just survive!

Science has proven that we only have the mental capacity to make a few good decisions each day. If we find ourselves making too many decisions in a short span of time, it can lead to what is called "decision fatigue." Decision fatigue occurs when people feel exhausted from making too many choices. Psychologists have found that, even though we generally like having choices, having to make too many decisions in a short amount of time may lead us to make decisions that are less than optimal. Avoid this by deciding once!

One of my greatest joys is helping others to get started on their chemical-free journey. Let's chat!

ELEVEN

YOUR EMOTIONS

Here are a few things that I've learned for ME. You must test your own boundaries and learn for YOU.

When I had my health crash in 2006, of course, the hormones were only one aspect of it. There were other factors that contributed to the crash, or at least I could list the stressors that may or may not have contributed to it but were affecting me, nonetheless.

There were things I could control and things I couldn't from both the past and the present, and I also slowly learned how my gut health related to my feelings and overall health. Thankfully, I had learned a few things prior to this experience . . . but oh, I've learned so much more!

Make Good Decisions Once

Making decisions is a constant in life. Sometimes, they're tough. Sometimes, they're simply based on preference, and there's no right or wrong answer. Those are the easy ones. Sometimes, our decisions affect others, and they may come back for a good ole blame game. Sometimes, you can make a decision once that'll free you from future decisions — like I'm never going to wear neon yellow pants. Easy. If that fashion trend comes around, I'll not waste a second on that decision.

This is a powerful tool when we're deciding on our morals or values. (See Chapter 2)

Own Your Decisions

After you've done your due diligence and made the decision, own it! Don't second guess it or replay the decision in your mind, wondering if it was the right one. A decision hangover can be exhausting and draining. So, train yourself to own your decisions!

You can practice this every time you go to a restaurant. Make your selection quickly, close the menu and own your decision. Even if you don't like what you've ordered . . . own it and learn from it. I've learned never to order margaritas in a restaurant because they're just not as good as the one I make at home. That decision I made once, and it makes the ordering process so easy!

Don't Settle

Have you ever spent the whole afternoon shopping, and at the end, you were empty handed? You still need the items you went for, and so you settle. You give your money for something you don't love.

Here's an example: You need a couch. You've fallen in love with one, but it's outside of your budget, so you spend hours shopping in the stores or on-line. Nothing measures up to the one you love. Do you settle? Or save?

Or worse yet, you can't find anything you love. Can you wait? Can you find another solution like pulling in some chairs from around the house? Then start saving for when you do find the one you love.

There's nothing worse than settling.

I'm not talking about yielding to your mate to come to an

agreement. I'm talking about settling for less than best because of impatience.

If I can tell you just one thing that was the most powerful truth that I've learned, it is:

YOU ARE ENOUGH

When your body crashes and you're just an emotional blob, YOU MUST KNOW that YOU ARE ENOUGH. This truth carried me and helped me to rise up and do what I could with dignity and grace.

Believe this every day. Protect yourself from messages that would suggest otherwise. Most people already know this about you. But you have to know this about you. Of course, this is not said with a selfish, me first slant, but rather, it's a gentle reminder that even though you didn't get it all done today, there's always tomorrow. Even if the to do list is growing instead of shrinking, and you feel like you're drowning in just the everyday. Sometimes just sitting down quietly and honoring what you've done can make all the difference. Reminding yourself that you've done your best and you are enough, is just the little hug that we all need to give ourselves.

P.S. if you want others to believe that you are enough, then you have to believe it too.

Control the Controllable

The only thing that is in your control is you. However, if you notice things that consistently stress you out, or bring you down, or you feel viscerally in your body a reaction to the news, or to social media, or a person or a situation, as the gatekeeper of your emotions, you can choose whether to allow those things to enter and/or affect you.

I personally find that watching the news doesn't make me

feel good, so I keep up to date by listening to podcasts. That way, I get the news without the graphic pictures to go with it.

Recognize the ebb and flow of your week. Like the waves of the ocean, we can't always be cresting . . . after the crest comes the trough, and then, there's the crashing on the shore. When that happens, we could think "what's wrong with me? I hate my life, and I quit! Why do I ALWAYS feel this way (on Tuesday)?" Or we could just ride the wave. Honor the cyclic nature of our bodies, emotions, earthly home and have an extra cup of tea on Tuesday.

Don't go BACK to High School

Remember the DRAMA? Why would we want that back when we've already graduated? If you get those old nostalgic feelings (of drama) from a person, a situation, or a social media feed, then what can you do?

If they're people, places, and things that you can't in good conscience avoid, then realize that you can't change others; you must change yourself. Reframe your reactions, your feelings, your boundaries and change your mind. I promise it works!

TWELVE

YOUR MIND AND SPIRIT

They say you are what you eat, and on many levels, it's true. The quality of the food we consume affects our energy and vitality, and we'll either be vibrant, healthy people or not. The same is true with what we put into our mind and how we shape ourselves as people. We have to be intentional as we strive to become better versions of ourselves every day. Just like your literal diet is made up of small choices every day that add up to either a positive or negative result. The same is true with the small choices that you make every day of what you read, consume on social media, TV and, of course, the friends you choose to spend time with.

Nest Pretty is all about making those conscious decisions to keep your mind clean and uncluttered so that you can reach your goals and be the best version of yourself every day.

Here are a few things that help to clear my mind of clutter when I'm feeling overwhelmed:

Brain Dump

Weekly, I like to do what's called a brain dump. I basically write out a massive list of all the things swimming around in my mind, and I write it in my planner so that this list goes with me everywhere I go. Ideas, to do lists, procrastinations, and then I prioritize them and start chipping away at them. Getting it out of your head and onto the paper frees you. It gives you a better perspective of what needs to get done and in what order.

Sitting Quietly

I have my most creative thoughts when I'm sitting quietly. I'll have a pen and paper handy to record my musings. It's also in these moments that I can problem solve my most pressing issues.

Edit Your Self-Talk

Do you find yourself often sighing, feeling like you're running ragged, stressed, always behind, overwhelmed or tired? Do you hear yourself saying things like, "I'm so busy," "I'm so tired," "I'm so stressed," or "I'm sick and tired"? If you're anything like me, you probably get tired of hearing yourself say such things to describe your LIFE.

What can you change in your self-talk? It may be that you just need to change your story! Get a better story or change your circumstances.

Here's what I mean:

One year, early in January, I did a year-end review. One of the questions I asked myself was "what am I willing to let go of?" I decided to let go of the story I'd been telling: "I'm still trying to figure everything out." This story began when our career of volunteer service came to an end in 2016. At the time, the story helped me to feel like there's a reason why my life felt out of control, why I didn't have the answers to the most basic questions, like where do you live and what are your goals? This story also served to give me some grace and patience with myself.

What I've come to realize is that EVERYBODY is trying to figure everything out!

By constantly telling this story, however, I was holding myself back from learning. As soon as I made the mental shift to change my story, I began learning all the things I needed to learn, and it happened quickly and easily!

So far, changing my story has served me better than the story I had told myself for three years. My story started out as a protection and ended up serving as a crutch.

I always know when a story is old — when I get tired of hearing myself tell it.

A story can serve to protect you, or it can move you forward. It can help you to deal with grief, and that's how it helped me. However, at some point, we have to change our story which is within our control and power to do! I think that's amazing!

Does this mean that I now have everything figured out? Absolutely not! However, I'm so happy where I am and can move on from here with a curiosity and a willingness to learn!

Protect your mind and the person you're aiming to be by being intentional with the small choices that you make every day!

It'll add up! I promise!

PART THREE
NESTING

THIRTEEN

CLEANING

So, apparently, 90% of Nest Pretty is about our attitude and how we show up in our life and family. This is Chapter 13 explaining Nest Pretty, and we are just now getting to my favorite part.

Cleaning Your Nest

Yes, call me weird, but I love cleaning! There's no other job that provides such a quick feeling of satisfaction and accomplishment! Cleaning windows ranks #1 and a hard second is vacuuming!

The problem with cleaning our nest is that it takes time, and usually, it takes the time that we would much rather be using in a different way like going to the beach, reading a book or generally resting from our otherwise busy schedule.

Therefore, I like to break up my cleaning into small chunks that I spread throughout the week. There's nothing worse than spending a hard-earned day off cleaning (as much as I love it.)

Make a Master Cleaning Checklist

I love to have a master checklist on my counter every week that outlines the basic things that need to be accomplished for the home for two reasons:

1. I love to check things off of a list!
2. I want everyone to know what I've done and what still needs to be done.

This simple effort of having a master cleaning list fosters a helpful spirit in the family and encourages everyone to help out!

Pro Tip: If a family member pitches in to help with the cleaning, be extremely grateful and appreciative. NEVER redo what they've done if it's not the way you would've done it.

Clean Your Home with One Product!

Because I care about the health of my family and I love simplicity, I clean with one product and microfiber cloths. It gets my home clean, leaves it smelling amazing and does so without harsh chemicals or artificial fragrances!

Happy Cleaning!

FOURTEEN

ORGANIZING

I think that people are under the impression that either you're naturally organized or you're not.

Many people put a lot of pressure on themselves to be organized. However, here's the thing, most people are organized; they know exactly where to find their toilet paper, they know exactly where to find their spoons, forks and knives, they know exactly where to find their frozen food. These are very elementary but profound forms of organization that you've already mastered!

Nest Pretty is about making small choices every day that add up to a beautiful life! So, think about your personal organization; are there small tweaks that will make your life more beautiful?

Here's another organizing truth:

According to the sage advice, you should have a place for everything and everything in its place. If you're having a hard time finding a spot for everything, it's because you have too much stuff for your space. That means you need to declutter.

These questions will help you:

- Is it useful and do I use it?

- Is it beautiful and does it make me smile?

If an item is in your home, it's taking up valuable square footage that you're paying for. This item must pull its weight by being useful and beautiful, not stressing you out and causing you daily angst!

If the answer is "no, I never use it, and no, I don't love it," then get rid of it, donate it, or sell it.

Notice how that feels in your body when you don't allow "things" to rule your emotions: the feeling of freedom, the feeling of pride of space, and the feeling of control!

FIFTEEN

SYSTEMS

Having systems is a must! It's a lifesaver, and it's brilliant! Whenever you feel overwhelmed by a chore or a task, just taking a few moments to brainstorm how you can make it into a system or a choice that you make once takes away the overwhelm and gives you pride and a feeling of being in control. Here are a few examples to try:

Deciding on a weekly menu can be a lifesaver. Knowing your weekly schedule and your weekly lifestyle and then plugging in menus that fit the schedule/lifestyle makes it so much easier to shop and know what to have for dinner. You'll feel in control of that part of your life. Which is huge!

Having a weekly chore list printed out on your counter is wonderful if you love to cross things off the list or for anyone who may wish to help out! This should include the one load of laundry that you do every day (at least). And it should also have your yearly spring cleaning listed if you choose to break it up throughout the year so that it's all done by spring. This makes springtime a Nest Pretty holiday!

Anything you can decide once and then put into action is literally the system of choice. There are certain things to do on the first day of the month for example: change your air conditioner filter, clean your food disposal, and replace the baking soda in your refrigerator and freezer.

If it requires more thought such as a three- or four-month rotation, then just put it in your phone or a calendar to remind you to stay on top of tasks that keep your household running. Literally, Nest Pretty is about making small choices every day that add up to a beautiful life and having a system in your family routine is so Nest Pretty!

Not only does it help you to stay organized, but it encourages your family members to also pitch in and help, which is so Nest Pretty!

I'm curious! Is there a system that you use to help you stay on top of your cleaning, organizing, laundry, and maintenance? I'd love to hear about it! Ultimately, we learn so much from others, so come over to the Nest Pretty private Facebook group and share!

SIXTEEN

MAKE IT PRETTY

Regardless of where you live or what type of home you live in, your nest is uniquely yours. It's by making small choices every day that you can make it a beautiful landing spot for your family.

Ultimately, if your home is clean, that is of the utmost importance and leads to the health of your family, both emotionally and physically.

If your home is organized, that will also lend itself to you functioning as an efficient family, reduce stress and save you tons of time.

If you can make it pretty that's even better! It doesn't have to cost a lot to have a pretty home. Here are your most powerful assets:

1. Imagination: Free with the exception of the investment of the time to dream.
2. Inspiration: Free and abundant. Hello, Pinterest!
3. Ideation: The formation of ideas or concepts — in other words, taking your imaginations and your inspirations and making them so.

Nest Pretty doesn't mean the SAME as a page in a magazine. That would be an expensive mistake that will leave your home lacking depth and personality. Rather, pretty means curating a home over time, including beautiful things that make you smile and are useful, sprinkling in memories, conversation pieces and layering furniture that is both old and new.

Though I love cleaning and organizing, what I love most is making a space pretty, useful, and functional. I love to make my home a feast for each of the senses: sight, sound, touch, taste, and smell.

The first thing people say as they enter my home is, "It smells so good in here!" I use diffusers in every room with essential oils. I confidently invite people into my home, knowing the lavender, peppermint, and lemon are going to smell amazing and will make my guests feel "right at home!"

My diffuser of choice was mentioned in Good Housekeeping! To get yours, you need to be referred by a friend! I would be honored to help you get yours. This is one choice I've made that has simplified everything for me, leaving more time to use my imagination, gather inspiration, and turn it into an ideation!

SEVENTEEN

SHARE

Doing all of this work to Nest Pretty leaves you with the freedom and ability to SHARE. Sharing our home with our family and friends brings so much joy and contentment. Layering your home with memories and whimsy can make for an enchanting experience for your guests.

The thought of sharing your home may leave you with a plethora of internal stories that may prevent you from doing so. If so, I challenge you to listen up, to hear the stories you're telling yourself and make the choice to change your story!

Personally, over the years, I've heard myself tell stories over and over again, and eventually, I get so tired of hearing my own voice tell it, that I make a decision and put it to rest!

Your story could be:

1. "Excuse the mess!"
2. "I can't have anyone over for dinner; just look at this house! I'm ashamed of my home."
3. "I'm too tired and overwhelmed to move forward."
4. "I don't have any money to make improvements."

Check in with yourself and listen to your story. What are

the words that come to mind or come out of your mouth without even thinking about it, when your friend comes to visit, or you have a surprise visitor? How does your story make you feel?

Remember, our stories and even feeling overwhelmed are a choice. And if these are preventing you from one of life's greatest pleasures — sharing . . . then, it's time to make a change!

Life presents us with many challenges, and these may result in a mountain of things to do in the home that may prevent us from sharing. This is real, and please, give yourself some compassion. But if you're tired of the story and you're ready to move on, then choose it!

Pick that story that you're most annoyed with, make peace, decide, and change it.

Need help? Book a mentoring call with me.

EIGHTEEN

NESTING WITH HEART

Love is the ultimate secret ingredient of Nest Pretty. It's a universal truth that when there's love in a house, it makes it a home regardless of square footage.

Love will also result in the ultimate chocolate chip cookie! I've teased for years that "love" was my secret ingredient, to my fantastically famous cookies, then I did a test of what my cookies tasted like if I made them with hate and haste.

Instead of patiently and mindfully adding the ingredients one by one after stirring by hand, and thinking fondly about the recipients of the cookies, I dumped the ingredients into a bowl (according to the recipe) and used a hand mixer to hastily make my dough. I also decided to say a few mean things to the cookie dough, while I was at it. I was completely shocked to see, feel, and taste the difference. They were no good! Seriously, the difference was clear!

So, if you're going to go through the effort to make chocolate chip cookies or, frankly, do anything in life, then do it with love! The same goes for making a house a home; decorating it and filling it with memories and whimsy takes time, thought, contemplation, maybe a few sketches, musings, some hunting, gathering, and LOVE!!!

Cleaning and organizing your home while kicking the chemicals to the curb is a reflection of the love and respect that you have for yourself and your family. Keeping everyone above the wellness line, both physically and emotionally, is no small feat.

Ultimately, every choice we make adds up, and it will be pretty clear if we're operating from a place of love or not, a place of patience or haste! Granted, circumstances and seasons will come through our life, that may be hard, difficult, or devastating. If our nest is built on a strong foundation of love, we can weather the storms that blow by.

Get my cookie recipe!

NINETEEN

NEST PRETTY IS A CHOICE

Nest Pretty is a choice. Bottom line. It's about making life happen, not just letting life happen to you. It's choosing to be a participant in your life instead of being a spectator.

I have a friend who blows me away with her fearless approach to trying new things. She's no bystander in life. No, she's on the field, playing the game, and having *so much fun*. One time, she learned how to STOMP with a group and then went on to perform in front of thousands. I'm constantly inspired by her intrepid spirit and her willingness to go out on a limb and do something new.

> *"Making small choices every day that add up to a beautiful life"*
> — *Heidi Gammill*

Stop and think about the power and energy that you could gain just by getting out of your comfort zone, deciding and then following through. Doing so will come down to our attitude. Are you excited? Are you ready to get to work? You should be!

You're just one decision away from:

1. Running a marathon
2. Feeling your best
3. Getting more rest
4. Fueling and hydrating your body
5. Supporting your wellness and emotions
6. Loving your wardrobe and enjoying getting dressed every day
7. Getting your finances under control
8. Making your money work for you
9. Having an organized home
10. Living your best life

Your life is a constant work in progress. Here's the thing . . . our days, weeks, months, and years will pass, regardless of whether we're accomplishing our goals or reaching for our dreams or not. I've had many years that were just blurs, and if it wasn't for my regular journaling or blog posts, I wouldn't have been entirely sure what I accomplished.

So, I highly recommend having a list of goals or dreams in each area of your life, a punch list, or even a bucket list that will keep you pushing toward the things you've always wanted to do. It'll make you save for that experience you've been wishing to have or accomplish those goals you may have never dreamed were possible until you broke it down into tiny, actionable steps.

Whenever I've chosen to do the hard thing, I've been so empowered by the way our choices truly do add up and make us stronger. Allowing us to accomplish things that may have felt were impossible . . . until we did it!

So, what's in the back of your mind? What goal have you been pushing away or burying in the list?

Choose. Do. Be. Live your best life. Nest Pretty

To work with me — www.heidigammill.com

THE NEST PRETTY LIFESTYLE GUIDE

www.ingramcontent.com/pod-product-compliance
Lightning Source LLC
Chambersburg PA
CBHW071631040426
42452CB00009B/1576